# LISTENING TO GOD

# LISTENING TO GOD:
## Lessons from Everyday Places

## JANICE KEMPE

Daybreak Books

Zondervan Publishing House
Grand Rapids, Michigan

Daybreak Books are published by
Zondervan Publishing House
1415 Lake Drive, S.E., Grand Rapids, Michigan 49506.

LISTENING TO GOD
Copyright © 1985 by The Zondervan Corporation
Grand Rapids, Michigan

**Library of Congress Cataloging in Publication Data**

Kempe, Janice.
  Listening to God.

  1. Meditations. 2. Kempe, Janice. I. Title.
BV4832.2.K418   1985      242      85-4364

ISBN 0-310-34822-6

Unless otherwise indicated, Scripture quotations are from
the HOLY BIBLE: NEW INTERNATIONAL VERSION (North
American Edition). Copyright © 1978 by the International
Bible Society. Used by permission of Zondervan Bible
Publishers. Scripture quotations marked (NASB) are from
the *New American Standard Bible.* Scripture quotations
marked (LB) are from *The Living Bible.* Copyright © 1971
by Tyndale House Publishers, Wheaton, Ill. Used by
permission.

*Edited by Pamela Jewell and Julie Ackerman Link*

*Printed in the United States of America*

85 86 87 88 89 / 10 9 8 7 6 5 4 3 2 1

To my Lord, Jesus Christ, who is directly responsible for every good thing that happens in my life.

To my mom and dad, who are examples of what a Christ-filled life can be.

To Jon, my very best friend.

# CONTENTS

# INTRODUCTION

This book is about listening to and hearing the voice of God. Many of us grew up fully aware that God spoke to us through men, the authors of the Bible, who then recorded His words. We hear these words explained, translated, and expanded upon by ministers and teachers. Some people even claim God has spoken audibly to them.

Once in a while a news report tells about some misguided person who has blown up an office or hijacked a school bus at what he perceived to be God's command. This kind of experience scares us and makes us wary of anything as ominous as communication with the Almighty! We believe He spoke to those who were trained to hear Him, but we're pretty much in the dark about anything beyond that.

Some think God took a vow of silence when the authors of Scripture put down their pens.

They figure He must have said all He had to say in the Bible and that now it is up to us to determine how to apply His words to our lives.

I disagree. *Listening to God* was written in the excitement of having heard God's voice. No, it wasn't spectacular. I've never had a vision nor seen an angel or a burning bush. I can't give a direct quotation. It happens simply and quietly. God speaks to me through everyday experiences. He organizes my thoughts and helps me see the parables of Jesus acted out in my own life.

Sounds easy, doesn't it? That's why I'm writing this. I want ordinary people like myself to be aware of this fabulous dimension of life. It is available to anyone who loves the Lord and who approaches life expecting to hear Him speak.

I get frequent messages from my friends and family by telephone or letter, but if I don't answer the phone or open my mail those messages don't get through. How ignorant I would be to insist that no one was trying to speak to me. It's the same way with listening to God.

We need to listen expectantly. There is a message in every experience. We need to look for lessons in our thoughts and ideas and be willing to share those thoughts and insights with others. What a shame to look so hard for the supernatural that we miss His clear but subtle voice in everyday experiences. What a shame to expect to hear God's voice only through those trained to hear Him and miss what He says specifically to us.

When God speaks to me I tell Him immediately that I hear. When I'm scolding my children or laughing at their antics, when I'm happy or sad, or when I feel the urge to call someone I hardly know or give a freshly baked coffeecake to a neighbor, I recognize the voice of my heavenly Father. He scolds me and makes me laugh; He gives me such wonderful peace and joy that I write down what He says so I can be blessed by it again and again. Comfort, healing, reassurance, hope, and incredible joy are available from God's inexhaustible source.

I wrote this to encourage others to see God in the everyday experiences of life. Listen for the lessons He sends you and be ready to be a vessel from which He can pour His blessing on others. It's an exciting way to live.

# Finding
# the Miracle

I hit the brakes as hard as I could when I saw her exiting from the entrance drive to the grocery store. She was lucky I missed her. Apparently she hadn't even looked before pulling out. Then, to top it all off, she had the audacity to block my lane while waiting to edge into the busy oncoming traffic. I noted my clenched teeth and white knuckles and wondered how a total stranger could completely change my mood in such a few short seconds. My thoughts, my emotions, and even my physical state were altered by this brief encounter.

I couldn't quite shake the edge on my temper as I finally made my way into the parking lot. After I had found a spot for my car I got out, slammed the door a bit harder than necessary, and began struggling to separate two shopping carts. I could tell what kind of shopping trip this was going to be.

Then I encountered another stranger. He came out of the store with two bags of groceries in a brand new cart. He pushed the cart over to me, picked up his grocery bags, and said with a smile, "Why don't you take this one? It doesn't even go crooked." I accepted the cart, managed a surprised thank you, returned his smile, and began wheeling my shiny new cart toward the store. I noticed once again how quickly my mood had changed, but this time for the better.

In the first aisle I saw an older woman struggling to avert an avalanche of fruit. Apparently she had selected the one orange that was holding all the others in place. A slow but steady procession of fruit was rolling toward the front of the bin, and her two hands weren't enough to stop it. I helped her catch several oranges and together we restored the mound of fruit to order. I made some silly remark about the same thing happening to me once, and we both went on with our shopping—but not before both our attitudes were visibly changed. The woman who had been so shaken just seconds ago now examined cans, bottles, and boxes with a smile on her face. And deep down inside I felt a growing bit of warmth beginning to soothe my recently rescued temper.

*It's you, isn't it, Lord? You're here in the grocery store, aren't you? I can recognize your gentle touch, your kindness, your smile!*

In another aisle someone had stacked the

raisin bran four high on the top shelf. A short man and woman had parked their carts nearby and were looking for the manager to give them assistance. "There are times when it pays to be tall," I remarked as I stretched to reach the boxes. We talked for a minute about the arrangement of cereal boxes and then parted smiling.

The whole trip became one experience after another of kindness and courtesy. As I stood in the checkout lane chatting with a new acquaintance, I was aware of the tremendous change in my attitude. I paid my bill, toted my bags to the car, and began the drive home with a spirit filled with peace and calm—a miracle. What started as a bad day had been completely turned around.

*This is nothing new for you, is it, Lord? The Bible is filled with stories of miracles hidden in bad days. Once Peter and his friends were headed home after a particularly bad day. They had fished all night and had only empty nets and tired bodies to show for it. Then they heard your voice, and by responding to your command found a miracle that changed their day, perhaps even their lives.*

*I wonder how many beautiful stories never happened because people didn't listen to you. How many times did you walk away shaking your head because someone chose to keep a bad day instead of listening to you and finding a* miracle? Is there a miracle waiting to be found in every bad day?

Thank you for letting me see you in the grocery store today. I confess that on some days a bad mood is actually enjoyable and I'd rather let my temper go than listen to you. Help me remember how easy it is to listen for your voice and find the miracle.

# TWO MINUTES

The two minutes it took my friend to make a phone call tonight changed my whole evening. I must have looked a little frazzled at choir rehearsal because he knew I wasn't as "all right" as I said I was.

The drive home seemed endless. I felt like a forgotten toy left alone on the lawn all night. Tears burned behind my eyes, but because the kids get upset when I cry I somehow kept the watery pools from spilling out. "I'll be so glad when Jon gets home Sunday," I moaned to myself. "These business trips seem so long and I get so lonely."

There was nothing worth watching on television and no one I could call so late in the evening. Then I realized that even my tears had dried up. Rats! I could have enjoyed a good cry. I decided I might as well go to bed.

Just then the phone rang. "Hi," came the

familiar voice. "I knew you were alone tonight and thought you'd probably be lonely without anyone to tell you goodnight. So, goodnight."

How did he know when to call. My uncried tears welled up once again behind my eyes, and his touch of love released them. All I needed was to know someone knew I was here.

*God, your touch is so gentle when it comes through a friend. I must remember to take an extra few minutes to make a phone call and let your hand reach out and touch through me.*

P.S. I love you, George.

# REACHING THE LIGHT SWITCH

"Mommy! Come here! Fast! Come!" I could hear the urgency in my daughter's voice, so I flew to her room expecting to find her in physical danger. Just inside the door she stood with her face aglow. "I reached the light switch," she announced proudly. She was growing and she had proof.

When I first decided to follow the Lord and experienced emotional and spiritual rebirth, I felt brand new. I found new meaning in old familiar Bible verses and songs. I enjoyed new camaraderie with long-time Christian friends. Everything was fresh and new to me. Like a hungry baby, I depended on those older than I in their faith to feed me the spiritual food I craved.

My first big lesson was realizing that my new faith wouldn't keep me from making mistakes. I had to learn to ask for and accept forgiveness for being less than perfect. I got a lot of practice right away because my temper was still short and blew almost as often as before.

The Lord had promised a new me—a better me—and I assumed that meant my temper would be controlled. He said the old would be replaced by something new and better, and He didn't lie. But it's a slow and difficult process. I am growing, though. Maybe no one else sees or cares about the progress I'm making, but I'm thrilled.

*Thank you, Lord, for the little steps you help me take and for the little victories. I know I have a long way to go, but growth is exciting when you let me reach a new "light switch" now and then.*

*And thank you for celebrating my progress with me. For a long time I thought I could only come to you in humility and repentance. But now I know you are as happy with my little steps as I am with those my children take. Thank you for making me feel like the center of your attention. I love you.*

# DISAPPOINTMENT

I didn't expect God to say no. Everything seemed to be going right, so I was sure He would say yes. He knows the secret wishes of my heart; I share things with Him I wouldn't dare hope for in front of anyone else. I give my dreams to Him, and many times He makes them come true . . . but not this time.

I don't understand. I'm angry about how things have turned out and, if I'm really honest, I'm angry with God. I was so ready to accept good news today. I was all set to be excited and happy and to call everyone I know. It's not easy to accept God's will when it doesn't coincide with mine.

I don't understand why things couldn't have turned out as I had planned. Is there some reason my dreams couldn't come true this time? My reasoning, my intellect, even my faith seem insufficient. Perhaps this is how

Paul felt when he learned that God's grace is our only sufficiency. I can trust God much more easily when I get my own way.

*Forgive me, Father, not for wanting something outside your plan for me, but for refusing to give it up when you said no. Forgive me, not for being disappointed, but for wanting so desperately to control the situation. Forgive me for suggesting that I know better than you what is right for me.*

*I stand before you, emptied by disappointment but ready for you to fill my emptiness. I know you hear me. I know your grace is sufficient, and I will wait. Amen.*

# MY JOB

Lord, when I am weary from the endless task of wiping grubby little handprints off the windows, furniture, and TV screen, help me remember that the smudges were made by the hands of your children. When I trip and nearly lose my temper over the toys that continually clutter the family room floor, remind me that the arrangement was made by a creative, inquisitive mind that you have placed in my care. And when the baby cries at three in the morning and wants to play, remind me that you have given me the ability and compassion to care for his needs.

Lord, I get so angry when my books are torn up or the projects I'm working on are accidentally knocked off the table. And I can be cruel when toys are not picked up or when a white Sunday dress ends up crumpled on the bedroom floor with a chocolate blotch on *the front. Sometimes I even yell, really yell, when it's time to go someplace and both children have taken off their shoes and socks to walk barefoot in the yard.*

*Lord, are you sure I'm the right one for this job? Sometimes I feel totally inadequate. Thank you, though, for trusting me to feed, wash, and hug these fragile little bodies. Thank you for their easy forgiveness and grudgeless love. Thank you for their constant questions and profound insights. I thank you for my children, Lord, for your children. Thank you for allowing me to mother your little ones.*

# GIFTS

Apparently I'm a slow learner because it takes me awhile to catch on to things. God must grow weary watching me bang my head against walls because I don't listen to what I'm told. Why can't I remember so I don't need so many painful reminders.

I like to sing, do artwork, bake, head up big projects, speak to groups, and be absolutely indispensable. I try hard to be perfect and admirable. But one day someone else wanted to sing . . . and she was good. Instead of letting her song bless me, I let envy, jealousy, even hate, begin to grow. My other talents didn't matter any more. I only wanted to sing. I tried singing to God's glory, but all that came out was a song glorifying me, and it wasn't pretty. It was ugly and it hurt, so I quit.

Once the devil works a little seed of hate into a person everything changes. My life went from happily busy to frantic. My motives for doing things at church, and even at home, became tainted. The joy was gone.

When I finally realized what I had become, I was no longer a giving or forgiving person. It was painfully obvious who had become the center of my life—me. I no longer did things for God's glory, but for my own. I wasn't happy. Selfishness is a lonely state of being.

But then Jesus came, uninvited and re-sisted as He was, and loved me. Gradually my focus changed from myself to Him. Little by little I began doing things again. This time I really was doing them for God. I tried to sing again, and it didn't even matter to me that it was shaky. It was the best I had and I gave it to God.

My joy was burning brightly again, and it was all because of God's gentle teaching.

*Don't let me be too proud of myself, Lord. Keep my offerings from being tainted by comparisons or jealousy. Take all my efforts and use them as you see fit.*

*There is such freedom in giving to you. I know now that my gifts don't have to be great in anyone's eyes but yours. I know now that some-one else's beautiful song can bless me as it is given to glorify you.*

*Imagine if all the birds refused to sing because their songs weren't as beautiful as that of one songbird. How quiet and dull nature would be without the cackles, squawks, and chirps of all the rest of the birds. What you have given each of us is all you expect in return.*

*Thank you for giving me something I can give back to you.*

# DANDELIONS

Dandelions! No matter how carefully I try to pull one up, I never get the whole thing. The root stays deep in the ground, threatening to grow up and blossom again.

But despite their bad reputation, dandelions are pretty little flowers with their yellow strands all tucked neatly into the center. And truly they are the most beautiful of all flowers when presented clutched in a child's dirty little hand. No one gets yelled at for picking them. Perhaps they grow only to be used and enjoyed by children.

Dandelions are ignored or attacked, never nurtured or cared for, and yet they always bloom profusely. They demand no pampering or special attention to yield their bright blossoms; they pop up in fields, in lawns, and between cracks in the sidewalk, even in the best neighborhoods. Can you imagine trying to grow them in a garden? They'd sneak through the boundaries and pop their sunny yellow faces up in the surrounding lawn. They would never stay put!

Christians should be more like dandelions. Our sunny yellow faces should be a reminder that simple faith has deep roots that are impossible to dislodge. Our vast number would show the world that even though we are not fancy or pampered we are evident everywhere, even in the best neighborhoods.

We should be as easily accessible as a dandelion. Jesus was. We need to get out of our gardens and jump across the boundaries that keep us where people expect to find us. We need to show our sunny yellow faces in all the spots that need a little brightening up— the crack in the sidewalk or the lawn of a country club.

*Lord, help me become like a dandelion with roots that grow deep, a bright sunny face, an appealing familiarity, and the ability to leap the boundaries that keep me from ministering to the needs of the world.*

# I NEVER REALIZED ...

Kevin was sick. His fever was dangerously high, and he wanted me just to hold his hot little body. The doctor said his kidney might be defective and that he would need a series of tests run. My heart ached. He was only six months old. He didn't understand what was happening to him. Why should he suffer? I would gladly go through it for him.

*And then I thought of you, God, and your Son. How painful it must have been.*

Waiting for so many hours in a room where each person bore a private load of fear made my own fear and pain intensely personal. I could hear Kevin crying down the hall; he kept calling for me.

Then I saw his little face. His color was drained completely except for the red splotches around his deep blue eyes. The yellow hospital gown with the cowboys on it made him look even tinier than he was. He reached out for me, and at last I could comfort him; but I couldn't hold him close enough to quiet his gasping sobs.

*Father, I think of you and your Son and how He cried and reached out, but you left Him alone and afraid. You let Him suffer. You let Him die! How could you abandon your child in His hour of greatest need? Could you possibly love me enough to sacrifice Him? I feel so unworthy. I never realized . . .*

When the doctor finally told us that Kevin's illness was not serious and that he would be OK I felt like dancing and singing and shouting and crying . . . but I didn't ever want to forget. I will hold on to this experience to remind me how precious my son is to me and how precious God's Son is to him.

*Thank you, God, for what you have done for me!*

# BARBARA

I thank God for my Barbaras. I am always aware of God's love for me, and I thank Him every day for the beauty He lets me see and feel and hear. But today I thank Him for a very special gift; I thank Him for my Barbaras.

The move we made this year was exciting, but emotionally exhausting and confusing as well. The Lord knew I needed a little extra TLC along with the lessons He had for me to learn, so He sent three very special people—each named Barbara—into my life.

My first Barbara teaches me about the kind of love that grows and is sustained by a shared past. She is dear to me, and it was a wonderful surprise to find her close to my new home! We had spent some growing-up years together and so we know each other in a comfortable way that doesn't change much over the years—a way that gives rise to the term "best friend." She knew me when I first knew the Lord and has watched me grow and fall and grow again.

I want to be like her—comfortable, non-judging, and ready to be leaned on. Old friends are a special resource, and I must make it a point to contact mine occasionally and remind them that no matter how busy, exciting, or scary life may get for us as we grow apart, there will always be a sustaining bond between us.

My second Barbara teaches me that it is all right to be needed and to need. With her I don't have to have all the answers or be strong all the time. I can share my joys or sorrows with her and not feel like a burden. I can go to her to cry or confess a mistake, and through my friend the Lord can heal my hurt. She is such a gift to me!

I long for my friends to feel enough at ease with me to boast of an accomplishment or share a sorrow. That kind of compassionate friendship is only possible when God's love controls our lives.

My third Barbara teaches me to laugh. She is more at home with herself and her life than anyone I know. She accepts the gifts the Lord has given her and offers them back without hesitation or excuse. Her laugh is infectious, and she touches me deeply with her beautiful voice.

I want to be like her in my offerings to God. Modesty and humility can be carried too far when they are allowed to hide the gifts given to us to share. I should be so delighted with the abilities given to me that I take every opportunity to use them for the Lord.

*Thank you, Lord, for your gentle teaching. You took three important lessons that I needed to learn and beautifully wrapped each one in a special friend. Help me, Lord, to hear your voice in each person you send my way.*

# THE BUCKET

My back is getting much better now that I've rested it for a few days, but the injury still affects everything I try to do. Being still is not an easy assignment for someone with a two-year-old and an almost-six-year-old who want to help!

Today has been like a bad joke! I awoke with laryngitis and a sore throat. This combination of ailments has made life more complicated than usual, so today I am learning about patience and perseverance.

Krista had left for school and it was time for Kevin's nap, so I settled myself into a chair with the phone, my afternoon's projects, and the coffee pot by my side. I was determined to give my aching back a rest from chores and my scratchy voice a few moments of quiet. I had no intention of getting up, for any reason! "Kevin, pick up your cars and trucks and put them in the bucket," I requested softly. It sounded easy to me. He set off to obey me, but a problem kept him from carrying through.

"Bucket?" he said.

"It's right there, honey." The bucket was less than two inches from his left foot, but I could understand why he couldn't see it amid the clutter of toys, trucks, and cars that surrounded it.

"Bucket?"

"Look down by your feet. See? It's right there!" He had to be able to see it! It was bright yellow and in plain view!

"Bucket?"

"Turn around and look behind you, honey!"

He turned obediently, two and a half circles, and looked behind him. By then, of course, he wasn't even close to the bucket.

"No, honey. Look on the floor by the book-case!"

He looked at me with the blankest expression I'd ever seen.

"Bucket?"

A strange mixture of emotions welled up within me. I felt like laughing. In fact, I was laughing! But I also felt like screaming!

"Kevin, just go over and pick up the dumb bucket!"

I must have sounded a bit less than loving, because his next question came with wide eyes brimming with tears.

"Bucket?"

That stupid bucket! Here I was, straining what was left of an already sorry voice, and completely worked up over a silly yellow bucket!

"I guess I'll have to come and show you myself!"

Anger and frustration must sound a lot alike in my voice, because when I hobbled over to pick up the bucket, Kevin collapsed in tears. I didn't mean to scare him. He tried so hard to please me but he just couldn't see the bucket.

Kevin went off to naptime with hugs and kisses instead of cars and trucks, and as I came down the stairs from tucking him in I thought of my heavenly Father.

I can't imagine His patience. He has watched His children for centuries—wandering around, trying to obey Him, but just not understanding how. Sometimes His commands are so simple and yet we stumble around—not looking in the right places, not understanding. Sometimes I get so frustrated. I know God wants to use my life, and I want to be used, but I just can't figure out what to do! I wish He would say, "I guess I'll just have to come and show you myself!" But then I realize He already did that once.

*Father, keep me from being discouraged by my limitations. Help me to try my best and to be content to be a small part. Even if my job seems insignificant, help me to obey you in doing it. Thank you for loving me even when my own lack of understanding leaves me walking in circles and missing the point.*

*Please give me the patience and wisdom to allow others to struggle and miss if that's what their growing requires. Help me not to expect more of them than you do.*

*Thank you for your patience. You are a good teacher!*

# FALLEN LEAVES

The neighborhood buzzed with the sound of leaf blowers and lawn mowers as people made the most of this seventy-degree October day. The kids were crawling after a cat through billows of brown leaves, and in just a short time I had gathered a big batch of the very best leaves to press in waxed paper and keep for a while longer. Leaves are wonderful things!

I suppose the blue sky and warm sun were mostly responsible for the feeling of love and beauty and specialness—the kind of day that makes one breathe deeply and smile.

What artistic genius! What wonderful scientific engineering to plan such a thing as a tree! The brilliance is fantastic! Imagine programming natural reactions and components into a living thing so that it produces buds and flowers, fruits and shade, and ends with a finale of spectacular color—and to make it happen year after year! My grandparents had days like this, and my grandchildren will probably sit someday in a similar pile of leaves.

I am glad that God's gifts of beauty are alive and on-going. His thoughtfulness is fresh, and these lovely colors were created especially for this minute. I see His magnificence, but I cannot hold on to it, nor can I claim it as my own. I must enjoy His beauty and creation each day when it is fresh, before that day's unique splendor is lost.

As I sit teary-eyed in this pile of fallen leaves I realize that your gifts, whether a flower, a sunset, a crimson leaf, or a human life, are to be appreciated in their own time. Each gift sings out in its own lovely way the greatness of its Creator, but trying to make them last beyond their own magnificent moment is futile. All things fade away, but they are constantly followed by more gifts. To spend time mourning that which has passed is to miss the glory of what is to come.

Thoughts of a friend who is suffering from pain and sickness have been on my mind a lot lately. His suffering seems so senseless, and the inevitable end of life overwhelms me with an awful dread. But in this pile of leaves, God's symbol of eternity, I find comfort.

I don't understand exactly what becomes of us when life ends, but I am assured of a life following death. I am content to know that all who have called upon Christ's name will spend eternity with Him. I can't imagine a place as lovely as heaven—a place where all of God's gifts return to flourish together—where every glorious sunset, every blossom of spring, every bit of autumn color, and every one of God's children come together in one triumphant display!

I certainly didn't expect to get a glimpse of heaven's glory in this pile of dead leaves! But I needed these moments to hear God's familiar voice assuring me that everything is all right. I needed to put things back into proper perspective.

*I thank you, Lord, for making me. Thank you for my grandparents and for my grandchildren, for the continuation of life. Thank you for making so many gifts and for constantly filling my world with new gifts—reminders of your love for me. Thank you for your gift of eternity. Just the thought of you bringing together all your children to live with you fills me once again with a feeling of love and beauty that makes me breathe deeply and smile.*

*Please, Lord, bless my friend who is suffering today and comfort him with your promise of eternity. He too needs a glimpse of the glory that awaits your children.*

*P.S. I suppose it's silly, isn't it, for me to want to hang on to something that is meant to be a living gift and then to fade away, like these leaves, when you are storing up all these treasures in heaven?*

# ONE MORE CHANCE

"Make me a blessing to someone today." The whole church full of people sang the song with enthusiasm, and I sang along in harmony. What a happy song! What a happy thought!

But that was yesterday. Today I blew a chance to be a blessing. The kids were only enjoying themselves, but their deafening noise was beginning to irritate me as I pulled up to my least-favorite intersection. Out of the corner of my eye I saw him. Smoking a cigar and looking like a plump pig in an awful toupee, he pulled up beside my noisy Volkswagen in his undented, pretentious Mercedes.

*You saw what he did, didn't you, Lord? Before I had a chance to turn, he squeezed by me on the shoulder and cut me off! You know how I hate it when that happens. You saw me shake my fist at him, didn't you? You heard me yell at the kids to be quiet. And you watched as I cut in front of that pleasant-looking woman in the maroon Buick, didn't you?*

Standing in the checkout lane with two kids at the grocery store wasn't such a great place for a second chance to be a blessing. At least I didn't think so. The woman who hurried to get in line in front of me didn't even have any children, and her cart was loaded with brand name items—no generics, no coupons, and even two magazines. She was pushy and rude, and her cigarette smoke was annoying. I had every reason to huff away to another line and let her see my obvious disapproval.

*That was my second chance, wasn't it, Lord? I blew it again, didn't I?*

I glanced back at her as the clerk rang up my purchases. Every stitch of her designer jeans begged for attention; and I certainly had given it to her. Some blessing I am. Our paths crossed, but I didn't fill her need. What's so difficult about a simple smile? That probably would have been enough to brighten her day. She didn't look as if she'd seen many lately.

*Lord, could I have one more chance? Would you try one more time to make me a blessing to someone today?*

# GOD'S GRACE
# IS LOUDER

Am I talking? My mouth is closed. Yet I hear familiar words coming from a high-pitched little voice in the back seat.

"We're late again! Why are we always late? Can't we ever get up early enough to be on time?"

I don't believe this! My daughter is scolding her dolly. Two and a half years old and already she has committed to memory my worst rantings!

"Stupid lady! Where'd you learn to drive?"

This isn't funny! I feel terrible. Has she heard those phrases often enough to learn them word for word?

"Come on, mister, ya gonna sit there all day?"

What if she plays like this at nursery school? How could I let her learn this from me? What else has she picked up?

Suddenly my face feels red-hot. My heart is pulsing in my throat as my mind goes back over each bad habit, each unkind word. What next? My public image isn't worth a spit in the grass if my private image gets out!

The rest of the ride was silent. As I pulled up to park next to another mother with a little girl, I turned to have a talk with my darling little recorder in the back seat.

"Mommy, that lady has a dirty cigarette!"

Of course my window had to be open! I thought I would melt into a little puddle on the car floor! There's no taking words back, and there was no time to avoid the woman. I had to get Krista inside or I'd be late for work. I took a deep breath and we began the long walk up the sidewalk behind the frowning woman.

"Lady, if you smoke you'll die!"

Wonderful! The woman doesn't look at all amused. My face must be approaching purple by now, and my underarm deodorant has long since stopped working. I squeezed Krista's little hand in an attempt to convey my message . . . "please, no more!"

"Mommy, you're hurting my hand!"

All day at work, worry weighed on my mind. What started all of this today? Will she ease off after our little talk or have I ruined my daughter forever? I'm some example! Am I really such an awful person? How could I think that no one could hear me?

Returning to the nursery school parking lot

after a very long day of work, I saw Krista's class outside playing tag. She saw me and ran to her teacher, then ran to me. We hugged and kissed as usual.

The teacher was coming. I knew it! I had this coming! I dreaded what she was going to say.

"Mrs. Kempe, I'd like a word with you."

I buckled Krista into her car seat and walked toward the teacher. I took a deep breath and noticed the hot tears already gathering behind my eyes.

"I just wanted to tell you what a sweet little girl you have. It's obvious that she comes from a very loving home. Have a nice afternoon!"

*Thank you, Father, for making your love louder than my mistakes! How often I feel your grace!*

# WHAT'S THE
# DIFFERENCE?

"I envy you," an unfamiliar woman said to me as we made our way downstairs for lunch after a meeting in which I had given my testimony. "You've had such an exciting life. Giving a testimony seems to come so easily for you."

I said thank you because it was the only thing I could think of to say in my shock. Exciting? I'm a housewife with two kids, occupied with all the routine chores that come with the care of a home and family. I seldom get out for an evening of excitement, much less a whole life of it.

I thought back over what I said that could have given her such an impression about my life. I had mentioned my first real encounter with the Lord and the thrill of discovering that prayer produces real results. I told about our move from the midwest to the east and how wonderfully things had worked out when we sold our old house and found our new one. Things went smoothly once we put it all in the Lord's hands. I mentioned some of the prayers God had answered. Nothing out of the ordinary. Nothing flashy or miraculous. What I said was a simple recounting of my daily life with God in recent months.

Then the second part of her compliment came to mind. "Giving a testimony seems to come so easily for you!" That wasn't always true! I remember sitting by the campfire at the close of a week of camp and feeling like I really ought to say something. Sitting silently seemed wrong, as if I were letting the speaker down.

I've felt that way in church services during an uncomfortably long pause while the minister waited for voluntary prayer or testimonies from members of the congregation. I'd sit there, looking down, trying to put together some clever words or phrases about my faith. I'd worry about what I looked like and what I'd sound like, and I would hope that nobody who stood up before me would steal my clever thoughts! It was like being called on in school to report on a book I hadn't finished! I was trying to give a first-hand account of something I had never had much experience with.

Things have changed since then. God has filled every day of my life with little understandings and blessings, and now when I have a chance to share what my life is like with Him, I hardly know where to begin!

What's the difference? Is my life more exciting than it was before? No. But God is teaching me to see the excitement that was there all along. The woman was right. I do have an exciting life!

*Lord, you are the difference! Learning to look for your messages in the dull, ordinary routine of life has turned things from black and white to full, living color!*

*Help me to show people that the excitement in a person's life is not something that happens from without, but something that happens from within. Help me to show that there is no reason to be a dull Christian. We don't need to settle for the promises of heaven's rewards. We can claim some rewards right now.*

*Thank you, Lord, for my exciting life! Your ability to turn a dull existence into a life of color is a secret too good to keep. Help me to share that secret with all who will listen.*

# THE PARTY

As I sat in church waiting for things to get started, I glanced at the bulletin, found the hymns and readings for the day, said a quick "hello" to the Lord, and then allowed my mind to wander. It wandered to one particular event, which I think may have been the Lord's idea.

I went back to our vacation with Jon's family in Florida. We are a close family and try to arrange vacations together whenever we can. This time there were fifteen of us sharing three motel rooms at a lovely place on the Gulf of Mexico.

Jon, the kids, and I were just finishing our supper when my father-in-law came in and invited us to his room for a cup of coffee before bed. When we arrived, the door was ajar but no lights were on. I figured the room was empty and that we would have to search elsewhere for our bed-time coffee, but Dad nudged us on. As I stepped through the door I knew something wasn't right. A hushed sort of commotion was coming from the corner and I felt someone's presence in the darkness!

Suddenly, the lights flashed on . . . "Surprise!"

Dumfounded, I looked to Jon for a clue, but his face was as blank as mine.

"Why?" we asked simultaneously.

"Are you surprised?"

Of course we were surprised. Neither of us had suspected anything, and for good reason. There was no occasion!

"Why?" we repeated.

"Well," my daughter began, "if we waited for your anniversary there wouldn't be anyone around to have a party!"

Dear Krista! She presented us with a beautiful, handmade card that read, "Happy anniversary Mom and Dad, Love, Krista and Kevin."

I glanced around the room at the faces of my family, most of them huddled together in one giggling pile on a double bed. They had gone along with Krista's plan and were getting a good laugh out of the whole thing. I looked from one pair of eyes to the next, until my gaze fell on Krista. She wasn't silly. She was dead serious. She was proud! This party was important to her. She loved us, and her whole motivation for this party was to communicate that love.

My mind was abruptly brought back to the

church service as the minister stood to greet the congregation and make the announcements. I looked around at the people who had come to this Sunday morning service and made a quick comparison between the party given in my honor in Florida and this one given in God's honor. I could see the different emotions in the eyes of the people near me. Some were happy, some sad. Some seemed preoccupied, some indifferent, and some tired.

I wonder what the Lord sees when He comes to His party and looks into my face? Does He see the blank gaze of someone whose mind is on outside concerns? Does He see someone more concerned with the mechanics of the service than with the guest of honor?

These services are a chance for me to express my love for Him. I hear words spoken about His love from others who know Him in a different way than I do. I get lost in the glory of music that is offered to Him, and I delight in the ways other people express how they feel.

How many of these services have I attended without even a glance in the direction of the guest of honor? I need forgiveness for all the times I've let the Lord come and go without so much as a greeting! I need forgiveness for being concerned about insignificant details of the service when I should have been centering all of my attention on loving the guest of honor.

*Create in me a childlike heart and excitement as I prepare for your arrival. Thank you for the gift of your church where I can come to give you a song or a prayer or a simple, loving gaze as I learn from you. Thank you for always coming to the party.*

# SUBURBAN MISSION FIELD

Life in the suburbs doesn't require much sacrifice, Lord. We live as if we were in a society of kings, taking for granted each luxury we enjoy. We read the mail and answer the phone; watch TV and go to the refrigerator for a snack; send the kids to their beds, their toys, and their own cozy rooms. We awake in warm houses and stand perplexed in front of closets filled with enough clothes for several people. You have generously given us food, shelter, luxury, and work.

But that is not true on mission fields where people are sick and dying. There Christians sacrifice the love of family and friends to offer hope, life, and survival to total strangers. In urban ghettos, Christians sacrifice their own wealth and well-being to supply money, shelter, medical aid, and emotional support for the needy. In anti-Christian cultures, Christians often sacrifice life itself to take God's

---

message of peace to people who only know war and hatred.

But what about the suburbs, Lord? Are we on vacation? Why have you put so many of us here? Should we all leave home and go to far-off mission fields?

People in the suburbs are well hidden—behind names, titles, occupations, income brackets, nice clothing, ample houses, and multiple-car garages. Yet under the makeup and designer clothes, inside the air-conditioned cars, and behind the palatial suburban front doors are people, and some of them do not even know who they are without the trappings.

If only they looked needy, Lord! But most of them are more sophisticated and better off than I am. Their needs aren't obvious. If they'd just come and ask for advice! If only their hurts and insecurities weren't masked by jogging suits and fancy cars. If only I knew what I could do to help them. How do I tell them that you love them, and that I love them?

Our job is subtle, but it is real—to love, to give, to encourage, and to tell them about you—and to do it well we need tact, creativity, genuine love, and patience. We cannot allow our own luxuries to defeat us.

Perhaps the reason there are so many Christians in the suburbs is because there are so many here who are being deceived into believing they don't need God. They don't seem to need anything! Even some of our *churches seem to lose sight of spiritual needs when physical needs are constantly satisfied. How tragic that so many people are close to free salvation and yet they struggle alone because they don't see their need.*

*Lord, give me a fresh approach. Fill my common, suburban life with an uncommon, Christian radiance. Open my eyes to the needs of my community.*

*Thank you for the challenge of this mission field.*

# GIFT OF LOVE

Each morning I play a silly little game. I lie in bed and pretend I don't hear any of the noises around me. I keep my eyes closed and try not to think about getting up for a few more minutes. Jon and Krista get up and begin their mornings, politely pretending that I am fooling them. My ultimate goal in life, at that time of day, is to sleep until 7:30!

Learning early how difficult it is for her mommy to come to life in the morning, Krista assumed responsibility for herself and learned to quietly turn on cartoons or fix cold cereal. My son is not quite as independent, however, and comes to me as soon as he's out of his crib to begin pulling on my arm until I get up and fix his breakfast. "I should fix Kevin's breakfast," Krista said one morning as I stumbled to the kitchen. I told her that I appreciated her sweet thought but that I didn't mind doing it.

That evening I did something foolish. I stayed up much too late watching television. The next morning I didn't have to play my silly game—I was out cold!

"Mommy, you've got to get up, FAST! You've got to get Kevin. NOW! Hurry!!"

I was out the bedroom door and halfway to Kevin's room in a frantic run when I awoke enough to ask Krista what was wrong! With adrenalin flooding my system and my heart beating in my ears, I waited to hear the reason for this early morning emergency!

"His cereal is getting soggy!" she replied.

Krista tries hard to do what is good and helpful and right. I love her for her thoughts and efforts, even if the results are not always ideal. She demonstrates in a genuine way how much she loves us, and it makes my love for her grow even deeper.

Krista shows her love in many ways. On my dresser I keep a paperweight made from a plastic chair coaster that has a picture of a beautiful three-year-old Krista in the center. My husband has a plastic fork embedded in plaster of paris that he uses to hold urgent messages, such as "I love you Daddy." These are some of the favorites in our rather large collection of our daughter's gifts to us. They are priceless. They are not polished or perfect, but they are the best she had to offer at special times in her life.

With this in mind, I dare offer my talents to God. He is my Heavenly Father, and I trust that He looks on my efforts as a parent would. He loves my attempts, even if the results are imperfect.

*I give my life to you, Lord—everything I do and everything I am. When I am given an opportunity to serve you, help me remember that you love the gifts your children give to you, even if they aren't polished or perfect. Thank you for the unique pleasure and freedom there is in truly being your child.*

# THANK YOU FOR MOMMY WHO SLEEPS RIGHT THERE

Two-year-old Kevin was excited about sleeping in a big bed. We were on vacation and he had full command of a double, pull-out bed in the front room of the cottage. This was his first time out of a crib, so he felt rather proud. But as night approached the room seemed strange and dark, and the bed too big.

"Please sleep with me, Mommy."

I hadn't planned to go to bed so early! My sister-in-law and I had a whole year's worth of talking to squeeze into a few late night hours of our annual two-week vacation at the cottage. The children occupied all of our daytime hours, so we were very protective of those precious hours after bedtime!

"No, Kevin. You go to bed."

There were a few tears and then another request.

"Mommy, you sleep right here?"

Figuring he was afraid of the dark, I scrounged up a night light to make his room slightly lighter. "Okay, now you go to bed."

From the next room I could hear soft sobs and a persistent "Mommy, I need you." I got him a glass of water, another pillow, and his favorite toy, but each attempt to calm him was followed by the same plea.

"Please Mommy, you sleep with me!"

Finally I went into his room and snuggled up next to him, and he began to say his bedtime prayers.

"Thank you for Papa. Thank you for Mama. Thank you for Jody and Brita. Thank you I miss my Daddy. Thank you for my mommy who sleeps right there! Amen."

Tears filled my eyes. I cried and laughed at the same time. For the next twenty minutes I cuddled and hugged Kevin, and he finally drifted off to sleep. As I slipped out of his room, I thought of my Lord.

I learn so much about parenting from Him! When I ask Him to be with me, He doesn't waste time trying to find a substitute. He knows that a real need must be met with a real answer, not a trick. He comes to me as soon as I ask, and I don't need to pout or manipulate to get Him there.

Kevin didn't need a light or water. He didn't need a toy or another pillow. He needed me, and when I came to him, his need was met.

*Lord, my children are so important to me, and yet there are times . . . so many times . . . that I give them substitutes for my time. Does that communicate unimportance to them?*

*Help me look past my own selfishness to the needs of my children. Help me to be as available to them as you are to me. Thank you for coming whenever I call.*

# SUZY

"I have something really sad to tell you . . . Suzy died."

How could I deal with such news? I had never before felt that kind of pain; I cried for three days. Could there possibly be a lesson in it?

We used to wear each other's clothes at junior high camp (for some reason that was a thrill for us as junior high girls). We had such intense fun during those few years when we were all trying to grow up. There were five of us: Ruthie, Dodie, Suzy, Meredith, and me, and Michelle for a while. The girls gave me a doll for my birthday one year and we named him GERJL, using each of our middle initials. The R was Suzy's. She said it didn't stand for anything . . . just R.

I remember laughing a lot! I guess that's part of growing up. Once Ruthie taught me how to whistle through my fingers really loud.

I caught on at about midnight! We were in cabin 11 and my bunk was right under a nice older woman who was our volunteer counselor. Could she ever move when she was mad!

Suzy always got asked right away for date night. We'd be unpacking our suitcases and she'd already have a boyfriend! She was always the first picked, the first kissed, the first one chosen for the winning team. She was that kind of kid, and I always envied her a little bit.

After high school, I moved away from home, and when I came home for visits it wasn't the same. We weren't close anymore, even though we kept up on who was getting married and having babies. Suzy served at my wedding reception. She had a baby girl just before my daughter was born, and she had another girl when I was expecting Kevin. Now Suzy was gone. She hadn't been sick. She was only twenty-seven years old. Her baby was only four months old . . . it just wasn't fair.

We grew up hearing about Jesus and heaven. We went to Sunday school and Bible school and camp together. We were confirmed and accepted into the church as Christian women. Our futures were secure.

I believe in heaven. I believe in security. So I guess I'm not really crying for Suzy at all. I'm crying for her husband and her kids. I'm crying for her family and her friends and for me. We are still here. We are still living. Suzy's taken care of.

How well I remember the Scripture that was read at my Grandpa's funeral! I went home and memorized it because it was such a wonderful promise: "Do not let your hearts be troubled. Trust in God, trust also in me. In my Father's house are many rooms; if it were not so, I would have told you. I am going there to prepare a place for you. And if I go and prepare a place for you, I will come back and take you to be with me that you also may be where I am" (John 14:1–3 NIV).

There was a place prepared for Suzy, and I have no reason to feel sorry for her. She's with the Lord!

*Thank you for the way you let the gift of a friend's life touch mine. Thank you that even her death can bring me peace. I'm not as afraid as I was before. My tears are still falling, but not out of anger or fear. The tears are in memory of a very beautiful creation that no longer is here, but that I will enjoy again one day with you.*

*Thank you for your eternal care.*

# LET'S CLEAN, MOMMY

"Mommy, will you help me clean my room?"

How could I resist an invitation like that?

It started out to be fun. As I sorted through the pile of clothes on the closet floor, Krista began making her bed.

"Mommy, how about some music to work by?"

She slipped over to her record player and began looking through her records for one that would pep up our work. Record jackets on children's records are attention grabbers, so five minutes later when I backed out of the closet with a pile of dirty clothes, I noticed Krista sitting on the floor, completely engrossed in her record jackets, her bed still unmade.

"Hey, wake up!" I began. "You aren't getting anything done! Now put on that record and go make your bed!"

---

She shrugged a quick apology, put the record on the turntable, and headed back toward the bed.

I started my next task—untangling hair ribbons that had found a place on the floor in the corner. It only took two or three minutes to untangle them and put them in the appropriate drawer, but when I looked back at Krista I was irritated again. She had found a naked dolly under her pillow that *had* to be dressed, so there Krista sat . . . on her unmade bed!

"I'm starting to get angry with you!" I huffed. "*You* aren't doing any of the work. Now put that dolly down and make your bed!"

She promised to try harder. As I began dusting, she folded her nightie to go under her pillow.

After the dusting, I arranged and rearranged the knick-knacks on the dresser. When I glanced back toward Krista she was nowhere to be found. Where was she? Certainly not working on her bed! Then I noticed something moving under the bed.

"Krista what are you doing now?" I pleaded. Slowly she crawled out from under the still unmade bed with three stuffed animals and assorted doll clothes.

"I don't know," she replied dreamily.

"That's it! You asked for my help, but that isn't really what you wanted, is it? You wanted me to come up here and do all the work for you, didn't you? Well, that just won't work, young lady! Only if you're serious about doing the job will I help!" I stormed down the stairs and left behind a rather bewildered little girl.

My goodness! What a reflection of myself! I think God even planned the dialogue to this one. It's such a clear illustration of my relationship with Him that I'm embarrassed by it!

Is this the way He handles my half-hearted prayers? How many times have I prayed "God, help me . . . " and then sat back and waited for Him to do all the work? I remember asking for help in overcoming a bad habit, but what I really wanted was for Him to wave a magic wand and remove my temptations and weakness. I remember asking Him to use me as a messenger of His love, when I didn't even try to be loving!

A request for help is worthless if I refuse to do my share of the work. Self-control can't come from Him unless it comes from Him through me! Forgiveness can't be bestowed on my enemies on my behalf unless I let go of my hate and resentment that needs to be healed first. Perhaps my prayers seem to go unanswered sometimes because God is a good parent. He won't do for me what I need to learn to do myself. When I ask for His help, that's what I should expect—help, not for Him to take over and do my share of the work!

*I thank you, Lord! I stand before you convicted of my laziness and aware that "you do it" prayers just aren't effective.*

*Help me to help myself. Thank you for insisting that I clean up my own messes and accomplish my own goals. I think that's good parenting. Otherwise I'd never grow up or learn to do anything for myself.*

# VACATION

Vacation is coming! I'm frantic! I need to wash the clothes, make arrangements for the dog, stop the mail, water the plants, and pay the bills. What clothes should I take? What should I take for the kids if it's cold? What if it's hot? What do I need to take along to share with my family? Who'll take care of our garden? I should ask the neighbors to park their car in our driveway so it will look as if we're home. I'll need to set the timers and lock all the doors and windows. And oh—the bank! It closes in half an hour and I forgot to get out some money!

Vacation. A wonderful time, but an awful thing to prepare for! And then there's coming home! Just the thought of all those dirty clothes and sandy toys makes me cringe!

It occurs to me as I chase myself around the house that heaven will be the ultimate vacation! No clothes to pack, no worries, no concerns for all the possessions that drive us crazy here on earth.

*Lord, thank you for keeping my departure time a secret! If I knew when you planned to take me, I'd make myself half frantic worrying about unimportant details! I guess I need to learn to be ready all the time. That's the key, isn't it?*

# TIME WITH DADDY

Kevin and I walked Krista to kindergarten today. Her school is up and over a large hill and through a woods, so we noticed each flower and green leaf that told us spring was near and listened to the birds that had returned after a long, cold winter.

The walk was fun, and Krista was proud to show off her little brother as they stood in line together awaiting the bell. He performed admirably. Krista got him to say every word in his vocabulary and a few we had never heard from him before.

After the goodbye kisses Kevin and I began our walk back up and over the big hill. He was fascinated by the selection of rocks and sticks and immediately began gathering a collection. Our progress was slow because we had to stop every few steps to retrieve dropped treasures. The capacity of his two hands just wasn't enough to accommodate the desires of his curious little mind! He had no more time for noticing birds and flowers. With grim determination, he tended to the safe passage of his wonderful new collection.

I couldn't understand why each stone was so special, nor why he needed so many sticks, but he guarded them with great care and knew instantly if he had dropped one. He was so taken by his new acquisitions that the walk home took twice as long as the walk to school. Upon reaching our front door, Kevin and I were both exhausted!

He struggled up the front steps and through the front door. But suddenly he let go of his precious treasures, and they fell to the front hall floor. His determined scowl melted into a wide grin. He ran off as if the things he had struggled to bring home had lost their value. Kevin had seen something far more important, and immediately his focus had changed to a new center of attention—Daddy!

I've seen this happen time and time again in our home. A day of play that couldn't be interrupted for any reason will come to a sudden and willing halt when a chance to be with Daddy comes up. It doesn't matter where he is going: to the store, the library, even the gas station, the invitation to follow is irresistible to his kids. Their toys, rocks, swing sets, and make-believe are all gladly forsaken for time with Daddy!

I long to keep in mind that picture of my little boy dropping his burdensome treasures to run to his father. I too get burdened down by my treasures. My house, my belongings, my responsibilities, and all the things I've spent so much time and energy acquiring seem to take me over sometimes. I find myself attending to their care with an overwhelming single-mindedness. Sometimes I need to see God and do more than just acknowledge His presence. I need to drop everything else and run to Him. I need to forsake the housework, the shopping, and the thousand other things that occupy my time, and go to Him for a time of togetherness.

*I am thankful that you are my Father and that when I run to you, you aren't too busy for me. The burdens and responsibilities of my earthly treasures won't evaporate before I've had the chance to attend to them. After we've had our time together, I'm prepared to assume my responsibilities again.*

*Thank you that it's okay to put everything on hold so I can be with you, like a child, every once in a while.*

# RIDE WITH ME, LORD

*Ride with me, Lord. We can talk in the car. I've already botched up a perfectly lovely day by sleeping fifteen minutes too long. I'm really wound up this morning. I'm sure I'll never make it to school on time!*

Some days this happens. I don't think there's any reason for it, but every now and then a day begins to fall apart the minute I open my eyes. Today neither Jon nor I could wake up, and when I finally realized I had to be to work in forty minutes, I panicked!

Poor Krista! She wasn't even awake yet and I was shouting orders to her.

"Wear your green-and-yellow shirt and your green pants. Try to find them yourself. Don't forget socks! Try to be a big girl and dress yourself today, okay? And hurry!"

I got the Cheerios poured, but there wasn't any milk. I checked last night and there was enough for breakfast. But no one will admit drinking it, of course!

And why did the dog have to throw up this morning? (And on the papers I just corrected last night!) I can't believe I actually yelled at the poor thing for being sick!

Why Krista decided to take off her green pants and put on red ones is beyond me. Look at her! Green, yellow, and red!

Now I'm sitting behind a stalled car at a traffic light feeling totally helpless and out of control. Times like these are when I need you most, Lord. I need you to come into my crummy little car and take control of my temper, of my anxiety, of me! I can't wait until I have time to sit still and have devotions. I need you now. It's an emergency!

I need your loving touch to show me the proper perspective on things again. I need to see my problems as challenges, and the people I meet as part of your creation; they deserve to to be dealt with gently. I need to see my little girl as a sweet, innocent child who is doing her best, and my poor dog as an innocent bystander. I need to give out some love and apologies—maybe even a smile. I need a smile for that poor woman in the stalled car. Her day isn't off to such a good start either!

Lord, I'm sorry I let myself slip into tantrums. I keep giving control over to you only to wake up late and try to start an already *frantic morning without you. I'm wrong again.*

*Thanks for riding with me. Thanks for not waiting for me to come to you in a fancy church. Please spend the whole day with me. I have a feeling I will need your loving touch especially today!*

# OUT OF THE DEPTHS

I'll bet I've washed that dish a million times! My kitchen sink seems like a hole that I keep falling into and can't escape from. I wonder how many spoons and forks I've washed in the last ten years? And the laundry basket. It's perpetually full! I'll bet I could go to the dryer any time, day or night, and find at least ten ragged towels, six wrinkled shirts, and twenty-three socks, five of which have no mate. The dust settles on my bookshelves before the dust cloth is hung up, and the stairway collects lint before the vacuum is put away. Who cares?

"Out of my depths I cry to you O Lord; O Lord, hear my voice. Let your ears be attentive to my cry for mercy" (Psalm 130: 1, 2 NIV).

Am I in the depths? Is this utter despair? I don't think so, but it is definitely uncomfortable. I'm having the blahs.

"Out of my blahs I cry to you, O Lord. Lord,

---

hear my voice; Let your ears be attentive to my cry for mercy" (Kempe 1983).

That's my translation! Sometimes I have trouble relating to the trials and tragedies that drove God's people of the Old Testament to cry to Him for deliverance. They make my own trials seem unimportant in comparison. But today I think God is telling me to stop comparing and to realize that the depressions and setbacks I experience are just as important to Him as the conflicts and moral dilemmas faced by people in Bible times. They were His children, and He heard their voices and led them out of the depths. I also am His child, and He hears my voice and will lead me out of my depths. God is as eager to hear my pleas as He was to hear theirs. He listened to them in their despair. He listens to me.

My Lord cares! He cares when I feel like a failure. He cares when I feel as if all my education and training have led me to nothing but a sinkful of dishes. I think He smiles when I mop up spilled milk at each meal. I think he smiles when he hears a resounding "Yuck" in response to a new recipe I tried. He smiles and gives me gentle words of encouragement.

*Out of my blahs I cry unto you, and you hear me. Send me deliverance, and help me recognize it when it comes. Help me to hang in there. Give me a funny thought, a friend on the phone, or a letter in my mailbox. Help me to look into every sinkful of dirty dishes and see your gentle, Fatherly care.*

# LOTS OUT OF LITTLE

I was a little too generous in paying our bills this month and forgot to save enough money for groceries! Nevertheless we are far from poor. God has given us a beautiful family, a wonderful community, a warm and supportive church, and always enough to satisfy our needs. We are learning, however, to to be good stewards of what God has given us, which means using our resources wisely and carefully.

What was I thinking of when I paid off so many not-quite-due bills, I wonder. This was a big month for birthdays and wedding gifts, and I guess I just wanted to take care of everything at once. Jon's check should have come today, but it didn't; so now we are in a pinch. The Lord will take care of us, though. He always does!

As afternoon approached I sat down to spend some time with the Lord. Refreshed, my mood turned to one of rejoicing. I searched my kitchen and found an abundance of flour, yeast, some fruit, and a little milk, so I used some creativity to put those resources to use. The coffee bread and rolls that I baked turned out better than usual, and so, with a real lightness to my step, I set out to give them away. The idea seemed rather crazy, but I felt like sharing, so off I went to visit three of my neighbors.

"Here!" I said to each of them, "I baked something for you!" I still didn't know what we would have for supper, but I was having fun sharing what I had. I knew we could get by on some fresh baked bread until Jon's check came the next day.

I settled down with a painting project and put supper out of my mind. After an hour, there was a knock on my door. It was my neighbor.

"Thanks so much for the bread!" she began. "I was in the Deli and I wondered if you had ever tried kielbasa?"

I answered that I had not, and with that she produced a little bundle wrapped in white butcher paper. She told me how to prepare the sausage in her favorite way!

How fun! Not only did I see the joy of giving all over her face, but I was more thrilled than I could say! This supper would be something special, not only because it was something unusual and new to us, but because it came as such a lovely gift!

After I had thanked her and she had left, I

sat down at my kitchen table to tell the Lord how amazing He was. I didn't get far into my conversation, though, because someone else came to the door.

There on my front porch stood my neighbor from across the street. I didn't know them well, and I had hoped the coffeecake I had given them that afternoon would help that situation. But I didn't expect such rapid results! In his hand my neighbor held a bag of beautiful, big tomatoes from his garden. Again, the joy of giving was evident, and the joy of my receiving must have been apparent too!

My precious Lord turned my hour of need into an experience of giving and joy for me and two other families in my neighborhood. How can I worry when He shows me over and over again that He will provide all I need.

"Consider how the lilies grow. They do not labor or spin. Yet I tell you, not even Solomon in all his splendor was dressed like one of these" (Luke 12:27 NIV).

*I don't believe you are an easy way out, Lord. I don't expect you to make up for my own laziness. But I do think you will take my efforts and turn them into blessings if I trust you. I believe you always give us plenty . . . but I think sometimes plenty comes in the form of energy or love, and not always as things. I thank you that you are so unpredictable, and that trusting in you is so surprising and fun.*

# ATTACK

In the middle of the night word came to us that Dad was having a heart attack. We rushed to be with him. Standing around, still in our night clothes, we watched helplessly as the paramedics took him down the stairs from his second-floor motel room and off to the hospital. Dad was joking with them about dropping the stretcher as they maneuvered the corner, and the smile on his face was a brave one. He must have been terrified, but his smile was meant to tell us not to worry.

We stood around and wondered what to do. Certainly they didn't want us all at the hospital. Until some word came back, we had to wait. We held hands and prayed. What else could we do?

Usually my prayers flow freely, but this time the words stuck in my throat. I couldn't make my thoughts come together even in silent prayer.

"Lord, be with Dad." Is that all I can come up with? Shouldn't there be something more? My mind raced back to other times when sickness had drawn family and friends close together and I searched for a comforting word or phrase to hang on to. What was it that people said to comfort and reassure each other? I didn't want to hear empty, pat answers.

"If it's God's will . . . " I never did like that one. Usually it came from those who were unaffected by the situation. The words always made my stomach turn. It was a pat answer that required little thought or understanding. "My God, is this your will?"

Tears of frustration burst forth and I could feel myself becoming angry. How could sickness be God's will? Is suffering His idea? If it is, I don't know Him as well as I thought. How do I pray to a God who condones suffering and pain? How do I seek His help if this was His idea? Am I to plead with Him to change His mind?

All these questions filled my troubled mind, yet I remembered the story of Job. He was a righteous man, but Satan chose him as a target to try to get him to turn against God and blame Him for his sickness. That wasn't just a one-time battle that was recorded in Scripture and never repeated. It still goes on today.

I'm beginning to see that even this hurtful

attack cannot defeat God and His love. According to His promise in Romans 8:28, He has the power to turn any situation into good for those that love Him and are called according to His purpose. I don't need to beg Him to undo damage because He gives only good gifts. I don't need to bargain with Him or show Him how this situation ought to be handled. I just ask Him to work in Dad's life—in all our lives—to turn this situation into good. I want Dad to hear the Lord say that this wasn't His idea, and that He's ready to help him fight. I want him to know God's there, as He has been all along.

The next few days were hard, especially for my mother-in-law, as we waited for some word . . . for healing . . . for anything! We were all far from home, yet people from all over kept calling and assuring us of their prayers for Dad. Many offered to help and some even offered us places to stay. The Christian love that surrounded us was wonderful.

After days of tests and more tests, the doctors finally told us what was wrong. There was a ninety percent blockage of a coronary artery; corrective measures would have to be taken. But what the doctor's didn't find in all of their tests was the most surprising. They found no evidence of damage to Dad's heart as a result of the attack. God was responsible for that.

God touched Dad's heart, and I am deeply thankful. He looked after our family in such a special way, and let me see once again that His help is available in every crisis. I'm thankful for doctors and friends through whom God ministered to our special needs, and I'm especially thankful for God's very special gift to me—my father-in-law.

> *Please, Lord, help me to be aware of your constant care. Thank you for your remarkable faithfulness and your willingness to stay close by, even when I'm angry. Be with all of us in a very special way. Amen.*

# NAPTIME

"Kevin, it's time for your nap," I said gently and positively.

"No!" came his reply. "I not need a nap today!"

For a two-and-a-half-year-old his command of the English language is quite good. He has no trouble getting his message across! He wants to be completely independent in everything he does, but unfortunately, he doesn't always know what's best for him—like today.

It's naptime, but he sees the other kids outside and all the toys he could be playing with, and the nap doesn't seem important. I know better. There have been days when we have foregone the nap for a trip or some other special reason, but the whole family pays for it that night! I know exactly what would happen if I let him skip his nap. First he would get crabby about supper time. Then he would fall asleep during supper and I'd carry him up to his room for the night. At dawn, when the house is still and all are asleep, I would hear his "little" voice screaming, "Mommy, I'm up!"

No thank you! It's naptime and that is that!

Getting him into bed took me some coaxing and caused Kevin some tears, but within ten minutes he was sound asleep, and remained so for two and a half hours. Sleep is a necessary part of growing, and no one, especially a two-year-old, can go without it without paying for it later.

I too am on the verge of having to pay for something I shouldn't have gone without.

I awoke this morning with a headache, probably because I knew an overwhelming list of things to accomplish by the end of the day was awaiting me. I got off to a good start, but I wasn't the kind of mother I should have been to the kids and I treated people badly on the phone. I've been a little crabby. No, I didn't forget my nap, but I neglected to do something just as important to my growth as a nap is to my son's. I skipped my devotions.

I don't always spend a lot of time in quiet study, but I do make an effort to spend time seriously thinking about God's Word and what God is trying to teach me. Today I was just too busy. (Martin Luther is credited with saying that he once had such a busy day ahead of him that he needed to spend three hours in prayer just so he could get through it!)

I had better take time to catch up on my

time with God before Kevin awakens from his nap. I need to remember that the time I take each day with the Lord isn't selfish time or lazy time or non-productive time. I need to change my ideas about chores and obligations. Before I tackle those, I need time with the Lord—time it takes to keep my spirit healthy.

*Lord, forgive me for neglecting my spiritual health. I know that is as wrong as neglecting my physical health. I also know that I must ultimately pay for neglecting either.*

*I love you, Lord, and I know that you know what's best for me. Help me to be an obedient child.*

# RIDING A BIKE

Jon and I bought Krista a bike for her fourth birthday. I enjoyed watching her eyes sparkle as her daddy brought it out of the garage. She wanted to try it out at once. The training wheels made the bike quite steady, but Krista was still too small to ride it comfortably. Her legs were too short and she lacked confidence. We didn't push her because we knew she was still small. For the next six months she was content simply to tell her friends about her bike and to struggle with it occasionally.

When we moved to New Jersey we no longer had the flat streets that made bike riding easy. For the next two years we tried in vain to get Krista on her bike and the training wheels off. She was still proud to show her bike to friends and to try it once in awhile, but nobody else around our house rode bikes much, so Krista was content to leave things as they were.

When we came back from vacation one summer, we found that two of the neighborhood kids had learned to ride their bikes. They spent hours riding back and forth in front of our house. Krista was content to watch them for a while, but eventually she wanted her bike out too. We watched as she tried to keep up, but the training wheels made for a slow ride and she wasn't having much fun.

One day she finally gave in to her Daddy's gentle prodding and off came the training wheels. She made a few short attempts that evening, but came in the house dejected and sad. She couldn't do it. But the next morning she was out again. With her Daddy by her side, Kevin cheering from the curb, and me running the movie camera, her first few feet of success finally came! She was off the bike, on again, then back off. She would start and stop, fall and let a few tears slip out, and then try again. She was wobbly at first, but by noon we were dialing Grandma and Grandpa to share the good news. Krista was beaming. "I learned to ride my two wheeler!"

This situation reminded me of myself and how God has helped me learn to balance and gain control of my life as a Christian. For a long time I was content to watch others and enjoy their experiences vicariously. I knew I had God's gift of faith, but I didn't really know what to do with it! Listening to others talk about their faith and being thrilled by their experiences can be habit forming. But what a difference when I finally tried to "ride" on my own! My attitude and my whole approach to life have changed since I learned to live and share and grow in my own relationship to the Lord. At first I was wobbly. I was off and on again. I fell a few times, but God always picked me up. The more I practiced, the easier and more fun it became! It's so much better than sitting by and watching others be involved!

*Today I pray for all of those who have the beautiful gift of life in Christ but are afraid to live it. Lord, help them to realize that not living the life freely available to them is like having a bike and never learning to ride it. It may take a little work and a little risk, but once they get the hang of it, it's something they'll never forget.*

# WORK OF ART

The sky is so blue and the sun is so warm! The trees are budding, and little green plants are popping up in my garden. The birds are fat, and their songs echo from tree to tree. A mockingbird sits on my chimney, and his song is piped through my whole house.

The kids are all charged up! Krista is swinging and Kevin is revelling in the dirt. I've been pulling weeds, clipping bushes, and digging holes for new plants; my hands are blistered and sore, and my nose is sunburned!

Days like this are priceless! I hope heaven is like this, or has heaven started here?

*Thank you, Lord, for this day! You thought of everything, and your creation is fabulous! I'll bet you'll even throw in an orange sunset to top it all off. You are the greatest!*

# ANSWER ME!

I can hear them playing upstairs. I know they can hear me as clearly as I hear them, but they won't answer! I suppose they think that acknowledging my call will mean an end to their play and the beginning of some responsibility. Of all the annoyances a mother faces, this one has to be one of the worst!

I walked into the family room and began complaining to Jon. "You know, it really bothers me when the kids don't answer! I know they can hear ... Jon ... are you listening? Jon!"

"Huh? Oh I'm sorry, I was listening for the Bear's score. What were you saying?"

"Never mind!"

My rational mind tells me I've done the same thing myself a thousand times. And mature, clear thinking leads me to conclude that anger is not the appropriate response to this situation. But my ego has been damaged! Am I so much a part of the scenery that my voice just blends in with the other household noises? The more I thought about it, the angrier it made me. I began slamming down the supper dishes on the table, and soon I had managed to work myself into a suitable tantrum. Great. This will make the whole family sufficiently uncomfortable during dinner. It's fun making noise! At least they'll know they've done something absolutely unforgivable. . . . Huh?

"Mommy! Answer me!"

I looked down to see my two-year-old son looking up at me with a fierce expression. He had been following me around the kitchen during my outburst, and I had let his little voice become just another anonymous annoyance.

I sat down on the floor and hugged him. "I'm sorry, honey. What do you want?"

"You called me! Is supper ready?"

He probably couldn't figure out why Mommy started to laugh and cry and hug him all at once. He probably had no idea why my miserable mood changed so abruptly. He could never imagine that he had just taught his Mommy a lesson that she very badly needed to learn!

*Lord, I hear you! Your patient, quiet voice coming through a loved one taught me what I* needed to learn. How do you manage to keep your cool after being ignored by so many people for so many centuries! How do you keep from rage when I let your voice become just another anonymous annoyance? Lord, give me the self control I need to keep a damaged ego from controlling my actions. Remind me that the faults I find so intolerable in others are usually the very faults you deal with so patiently in me. Give me the patience to be kindly persistent, and teach me to listen more carefully.

# LOST AND FOUND

On a scale of one to ten, with ten being ecstasy and one being a root canal without anesthesia, I would rank grocery shopping with two kids, hundreds of poorly clipped coupons, and never quite enough cash about two. My mood, no matter how cheery the outing begins, usually disintegrates to miserable by the time I get children, groceries, and fifty pounds of Dog Chow into the Volkswagen. Poor kids! They must fight tears when they learn another fun-filled hour at the grocery store is on the day's agenda!

I am amazed, though, that often during my all-time-least-favorite chores, God touches me with a warm and gentle insight.

Usually Kevin rides in the cart, but on one particular day he decided to push it instead. Being only eighteen months old, he didn't understand that the object of the game was not to push the cart into people and canned goods.

Krista was being quite helpful. She held the coupons and kept me informed as to which products are really better tasting—in the exact words of her favorite television commercials.

The fresh produce and cereal aisles went rather smoothly, but somewhere between the coffee and the soup, Krista wandered off. I didn't notice at first because I was busy trying to abort Kevin's attempt to ram into an elderly gentleman who was bending over to examine boxes of tea. But then I heard her terror-filled voice . . . "Mommy!"

Lost amid strangers and their carts and running through mazes of tissue paper and catsup, Krista's ability to think clearly had evaporated. She just wanted Mommy to find her. The weight of being lost and alone was too heavy to bear.

After an unsuccessful attempt to find Krista, I decided to remain in the long aisle that runs the length of the store. From there I could keep an eye on a good deal of the store as well as the information desk and the front door. There Kevin and I waited to be found. It may have been only two minutes or so, but it seemed like ages! My heart ached for my little girl and the panic of being lost that I knew she was feeling.

Suddenly a tear-streaked face flashed with recognition, and Krista ran toward me and the wonderful safe embrace that awaited her. "Mommy, you lost me!"

How confusing being lost can be, and how clearly I remember being lost myself. I remember anxiously searching the faces in a crowd for my mom or dad when I was little, and that awful lost feeling. More recently I remember being lost from the Lord. I remember wandering away and searching frantically for someone or something that could bring me back. I remember getting a glimpse of the Lord in the face of a girl who was trying to help lost kids like me find our way back to Him, and I remember running back into that wonderful safe embrace. Ah, to be found!

I've become so comfortable and safe in my closeness to Christ that I hardly ever think about the terror of being lost. I forget that there are people all around me who are searching and bearing that awful weight of aloneness.

*Dear Lord, sensitize me to the lost! Make my face reflect your countenance, Father, so those who are lost will recognize me as part of your family and catch a glimpse of your love through me. Allow me to share with them the joy of being found. Being lost is such an awful thing!*

# THE OWNER'S MANUAL

I can't believe how easy baking bread is with my *Kitchen Center!* It has a mixer, bread hooks for kneading bread, a food processor for slicing anything in a jiffy, a grinder, and a blender. I don't use it very often for fancy cooking, probably because I'm not a fancy cook, but at least twice a week it makes baking bread a real breeze. If I've had a bad day, or if my temper is on the verge of exploding, I knead the dough by hand. I punch it and hit it until it's nice and smooth. Then I wait while all my anxiety and anger bakes away. Most of the time, however, I let the machine do the work while I type or paint or do something else.

For the first few years after Jon bought the machine for me, it sat in my cupboard until I needed a mixer. Then out it would come for that specific job. When I was done I put it neatly away until something else needed mixing. I had a lovely, do-it-all *Kitchen Center*, no doubt about that! But I chose to limit it to one function, mixing.

One day I came across the owner's manual. As I began to read it, it dawned on me what I had available for my use in my very own cupboard! In that little book was an array of pictures and ideas that made my mind spring into action. Before long I had the machine out and was trying all kinds of new things. Reading the directions gave me a whole new insight into something I thought I knew all about!

The parallel to my spiritual life is remarkably clear! How lucky I am that God talks to me in such simple and illustrated ways that I can't help but understand!

Once I was given a brand new faith that was reputed to be something that could change my whole life. All I wanted, however, was something to fall back on when I needed it. So I kept my faith in a comfortable place and took it out only on special occasions: to take with me to church or to use when I got into a discussion with other Christians. If depression got a hold on me I could use my faith to help me out. I had a nice, convenient faith, no doubt about that! But I chose to limit its function.

Then I began to look into the owner's manual, the Bible. And there God was! Wow! I had no idea what things I could do with my faith! Miracles? Growth? Excitement? Is that how prayer is supposed to work? Amazing!

Imagine, I had a new faith and yet had continued to live as I always had! Accepting Christ was only the beginning. What child, after being given a ticket to Disney World, would be content to play baseball or jump rope just inside the main gate? None that I know. But that was how I was living. I was content with the ordinary in the land of the extraordinary. I was missing all the potential that life in Christ had to offer. Like the child at Disney World, I had to expend a little of my own energy and make use of my ticket or my visit would remain uneventful, dull, and disappointing.

*Lord, never let me put my faith away. If it is just a convenience I take out when it's needed, I will never get the practice and experience necessary to make life in Christ complete.*

*Thank you, Lord, for all the possibilities you have put into a life of faith. Thank you for providing the directions and power to make the promises in your Word come true.*

# JUST A LITTLE CUT

I am sure the woman wouldn't have said what she did had she known I was within earshot. Her words took me by surprise and left me wondering how to react. It wasn't a big thing. It was just a comment, a little joke about me, but it still hurt. I left the room, not wanting anyone to know that I had heard the comment or that such a silly thing would upset me. I returned after regaining my smile.

I've gone over that event in my mind again and again. I can't believe that a friend would say something unkind about me to someone else. Had she said it to *me*, I wouldn't have taken any offense at all, but she didn't even know I was there. And what of my other friends? Was it so funny that none of them could follow it up with a nice word or a disclaimer of some sort? At least then I wouldn't have jumped to the conclusion that everyone agreed with her!

Was I being touchy? Or too sensitive? I don't think so. Once again I found myself in God's classroom learning about myself.

My mind flashed back and the Lord brought to my mind some jokes and remarks I had dropped in conversation, not meaning to hurt anyone. How many times had I unintentionally crushed an ego or made someone feel small? I was unaware how awful it felt to be on the receiving end of an unkind word or a critical remark, even a little one.

*Help me remember, Lord, how much a little cut can hurt. Whenever I am tempted to make a funny but critical remark, whenever I am tempted to gain approval at the expense of someone else's feelings, make me remember the times I've been hurt.*

# A HOLIDAY AT HOME

Today is rainy and cold. The leaves have passed their peak of autumn color and now a blanket of brown hides any life that remains in the flowers after the frost. Everything is bleak!

Days like this make me want to go home—home to Mom and Dad. Days like this even make me hungry—hungry for the tastes of home. I want something so specific that I can close my eyes and imagine every little detail of the things I feel empty without today.

I can feel the warmth of the air in the room. My father has a fire burning in the fireplace and I am sitting in his chair with my feet curled beneath me as I talk with Mom. She is busy stirring the contents of one of the many pots on her stove. Good smells are sneaking out of the oven, and aluminum foil packages scattered over the counter top hide delicious breads and treats my sisters have brought.

The muffled sounds of a football game on TV, accompanied by an occasional outburst, come from the recreation room downstairs. Someone is playing the organ in the living room. From all corners of the house come noises of different conversations mingled with the laughter of one of the little kids being tickled. Next to me at the dining room table the dishes are standing ready to be put on the table as soon as the board game being played there is over. Brief eruptions of laughter every few minutes punctuate the otherwise quiet conversation I am having with Mom, and every so often someone new wanders into the room, reminding me that this house is full of people I love.

Such commotion! Such wonderful, peaceful, warm commotion! I am so homesick today!

On days like these I don't feel much like an adult. I don't feel like a wife and mother. I feel like a little girl who needs to be in her parents' home, surrounded by that wonderful commotion. I need to be surrounded by people who really know me—who know every little thing in my past—and who understand, without asking, how I feel. I need people who can see the laughter and the tears in my stories without me having to be so painfully obvious. I need to be part of a family of people who know me—really know me.

I wonder how the first Christians felt as they traveled to strange parts of the world. The apostle Paul, who went from one rough situation to another and from one strange country to another, must have had days like these. The desire for home and family and familiar things must have ached within him at times, and he must have grown weary of being a stranger.

God promised never to forsake His children. But today I find comfort in another passage. Perhaps it was on a particularly lonely day that God gave Paul the beautiful words about love found in 1 Corinthians 13. The conclusion of the piece is perfect for me today.

"Now we see but a poor reflection as in a mirror; then we shall see face to face. Now I know in part; then I shall know fully, even as I am fully known" (1 Corinthians 13:12 NIV).

I have been promised that I will be with the Lord someday. But beyond that, I have a promise that things will make sense, and that I will belong to a large and loving family. What a homecoming awaits us in heaven. A place to know and be known. A place to understand and be understood. A place even more wonderful than the one I can't get out of my mind on this rainy holiday!

*Lord, you know and accept me just as I am. Help me feel your presence today, and let my moments with you satisfy my loneliness. Give me a sense of contentment with the way things are, and help me concentrate on creating a loving and warm atmosphere in my own home for my husband and children.*

*I like being part of a family. I find excitement in the thought of family get-togethers, and I thank you that the bits of heaven you have given me throughout my life are just samples of what is to come. Thank you, Lord, for knowing me and my needs. Thank you for bringing back into this bleak and rainy day a feeling of happiness and warmth, of safety and home.*

*I love you, Father.*